LEARNING
for the
Christian
family
ABOUT SEX

Sex
& the
New You

D1113513

For **young women**
ages **13–15**

CONCORDIA PUBLISHING HOUSE · SAINT LOUIS

For Discussion or Individual Use

Book 4 of the
Learning About Sex Series for Girls

The titles in the series:

Book 1: *Why Boys and Girls Are Different*

Book 2: *Where Do Babies Come From?*

Book 3: *How You Are Changing*

Book 4: *Sex and the New You*

Book 5: *Love, Sex, and God*

Book 6: *How to Talk Confidently with Your Child about Sex*

Acknowledgments

We wish to thank all medical, child development, and family life consultants who have assisted in the development, updating, and revising of the Learning About Sex series.

Copyright © 1982, 1988, 1995, 1998, 2008 Concordia Publishing House
3558 S. Jefferson Ave., St. Louis, MO 63118-3968.
1-800-325-3040 • www.cph.org

From text originally written by Richard Bimler

1 2 3 4 5 6 7 8 9 10   17 16 15 14 13 12 11 10 09 08

Contents

Editors' Foreword

This book is one in a series of six designed to help parents communicate biblical values to their children in the area of sexuality. *Sex and the New You* is the fourth book in the series. It is written especially for girls ages 13 to 15 and, of course, for the parents, teachers, and other concerned grown-ups who may want to discuss the book with the children in their care.

Like its predecessor, the new Learning about Sex series provides information about the social-psychological and physiological aspects of human sexuality. Moreover, it does so from a distinctively Christian point of view, in the context of our relationship to the God who created us and redeemed us in Jesus Christ. The series presents sex as another good gift from God, which is to be used responsibly.

Each book in the series is graded—in vocabulary and in the amount of information it provides. It answers the questions that children at each age level typically ask.

Because children vary widely in their growth rates and interest levels, parents and other concerned adults will want to preview each book in the series, directing each child to the next graded book when she is ready for it.

Ideally this book is part of a much more broadly focused yet more personal training of young girls for biblical womanhood. Young women grow and blossom into Christian womanhood through the teaching, training, and example provided by older women. God's plan for the growth and maturation of a godly woman unfolds as each generation in succession passes on the truths God imparts through His Word and the wisdom that comes as challenges are met and overcome by the power of God's grace through Jesus Christ, our Savior and Lord.

Use this and the other books in the series to facilitate your conversations about sex and sexual issues and when answering other questions a child might have.

The books in this series also can be used as mini units or as part of another course of study in a Christian school setting. Whenever the books are used in a class setting, it is important to let the parents know beforehand, since they have the primary responsibility for the sex education of their children. If used in a classroom setting, the books in this series are designed for separate single-gender groups, the setting most conducive to open conversations about questions and concerns.

While parents will appreciate the help of the school, they will want to know what is being taught. As the Christian home and the Christian school work together, Christian values in sex education can be more effectively strengthened.

The Editors

1

You've Heard and You've Wondered

How does a girl get pregnant?

What is a homosexual?

Am I normal?

Will my breasts ever develop?

You've heard questions like those on page 5 before—maybe you've asked them yourself. And maybe you haven't been quite sure about the answers.

This book has been written to help you answer some of the questions you have about your body, about getting along with others, and about gender differences and sexuality.

More important, this book won't ever let you forget who gave you life and made you what you are. You are a child of God. Because God loves you, He sent His own Son to live and die for you. This kind of love means He won't ever ignore you; He'll guide you and protect you and forgive you. Because Christ died for you and paid the penalty for your sins, God is able to accept you just as you are. And because Christ became a human being, He understands your questions about sex, your wonderings about your body, and your sexual daydreaming. He helps you to grow in a healthy relationship with Him, with other people, and with yourself.

He helps you to become a "new you."

Of course, reading this book won't automatically solve all your problems. You may still be disappointed with your body, the way you look, or the way you feel. But you will have the chance to look honestly at these things and to think and talk about them. You may wish you were different, but you will hear again and again that you were made by God.

On this page and the next are a few more of the questions people your age ask. On the next page are some places for writing in your own additional questions. Take a moment now to write them in if you want to. Then, when you've finished the book, come back to see whether they have been answered.

Is it wrong to read romance novels?

How are babies born?

Questions I Wonder About

Why don't I feel good about myself?

What happens when I have my period?

2

You're a Special Young Woman!

"Am I normal?" many young people ask. It's so easy to feel alone and different. It's easy to think that you are the only person feeling the way you do—about your body, your family, yourself. Maybe you feel this way because of the changes in your body. You may feel this way because your body is not growing as rapidly as other girls around you. Or perhaps your body is way ahead of the pack, and that doesn't feel so good either. Perhaps you are experiencing a growing awareness of sexual thoughts and feelings. You wonder: Are such thoughts normal?

It's good to have a friend you can talk with when you're not feeling good about yourself or are confused or puzzled. But it's especially great to know Jesus as our Friend! He can actually "sympathize with our weaknesses," the Bible reminds us, because He was "tempted in every way, just as we are—yet was without sin" (Hebrews 4:15). He really *knows* how we feel, because He was born and grew and went through the teen years too. That's why we can talk to Him and know He'll understand.

Even more, as your Savior, He can really help! He lived and died and rose again to make you a child of the heavenly Father. He's living proof that "the Father Himself loves you" (John 16:27). That's good to remember when you're feeling unlovable or guilty or anxious or scared.

In what ways has God made you different from anyone else in the world?

The God who loves you and forgives you is the same God who made you. No one else—not even an identical twin—is exactly like you. You are special; you are not a carbon copy of someone else. You look different, you feel different, you think differently than anyone else. You grow at a different rate—maybe in spurts, maybe at a fairly regular pace. But whatever your growth pattern, it's just right for you because God made you and set your pattern into motion. When you accept that, you can accept a lot of the other things about yourself.

So don't quit on yourself! Don't give up hope and quit trying. Perhaps you won't ever be the glamorous model you wish you could be, but you can do a lot with what you've got. Once you accept yourself as you are and decide you're worth taking care of, ask yourself the following questions. The answers you give will suggest what you can do to take care of your body—and your feelings about yourself.

1. How much sleep do I get each night? Do I sometimes harm my body with a lack of rest? How can I improve on this?
2. What are my eating habits? Do they hinder the growth of my body or help it? Am I a junk food addict, or do I eat good, solid, nourishing food? Do I sometimes eat too little or too much? What can I do to help my body by changing some of my eating habits?
3. Are some of my complexion problems caused by what I eat? And do I wash often enough to keep my skin from being too greasy and oily? Should I see a doctor about my skin problems?
4. What about exercise? Is my body mistreated with too much jogging and too much exertion? Or do I get most of my exercise sharpening my pencil or falling out of bed?
5. What are my feelings about smoking? Do I think that doing it will make me one of the group? Or do I take seriously the studies that show the harm and danger in smoking? Am I or will I become one of those teens who smoke, even though it is a fact that smoking is harmful to me and to those around me?
6. And what about drugs? And alcohol? Do I abuse my body by taking drugs and drinking alcohol?

To which of the following do you relate?

"What is happening to my body?"
"Why isn't my body changing yet?"
"I feel like I am too tall."
"I feel like I am too short."
"I'm so awkward! I keep tripping over my feet!"
"I'm so awkward! I keep tripping over my tongue!"
"My face has zits."
"No one else has the problems I have; no one ever did."
"No one understands me."
"I don't understand me."

How do you know you are special to Jesus?

Even if your answers show that you sometimes misuse your body and don't show the concern about it you might, God cares. After all, He formed your body and programmed it to work in a certain way, and He gave you common sense to take care of it. Sure, you forget now and then, but He doesn't. Remember, He's got quite an investment in you. "Do you not know that your body is a temple of the Holy Spirit, who is in you, whom you have received from God? You are not your own; you were bought at a price. Therefore honor God with your body," writes St. Paul (1 Corinthians 6:19–20).

Even if your complexion is poor right now, even if you're a bit overweight, even if you're carrying a physical handicap every moment of the day, you are His, and He's proud of that. Peek in the mirror again. Go ahead—it won't hurt. Look beyond the familiar surface and find the hand of God there. See if you don't feel a little different now—maybe even a little proud. Remember, you are a "work in progress." God is changing you into an adult. But He's not done with you yet!

How do you honor God in the care of your body?

3
Gender Is More Than Body Parts

People can get very confused about the word *sex*. It can mean either "gender" or "intercourse." Many people use *sex* to refer to the act of intercourse or to physical attraction between women and men. Basically, gender—whether a person is male or female—is determined by the type of reproductive body parts the individual has.

For Christians, however, gender involves more than just body parts. It's how we feel about and use our body parts as good gifts of God. And certainly there's no reason to consider any part of our body as dirty or unmentionable.

Even a child who knows the proper names for those parts needs to learn when and where to use the names. Many people use nicknames for *penis* or *vagina* in vulgar stories or jokes. But that doesn't mean these parts are dirty. How could anything God made be dirty? It's the misuse and abuse of these body parts that is wrong. Thanking God for your body includes thanking Him for everything that makes you who you are—your vagina and breasts as well as your eyes and ears.

When God first created people, He made them perfect. That means their bodies were perfect—every part of their bodies. God Himself said all His creation was "good." (See Genesis 1:31.) Take a moment now to look at your hand. Open and close your fingers slowly. Note the precision with which they move—instantly, simply on the command of your mind. What machine can be so gentle and yet as strong as a human hand? Picture the marvelous things that hands can do: dribble a basketball or move over a keyboard. Think of a surgeon's hands, skillfully manipulating instruments in open-heart surgery or a mother's hands, gently stroking her baby's fevered face.

> What are some wonderful parts of your body that you thank God for?

How does your regard for body parts such as hands and eyes differ from the way you regard the "unpresentable" parts of your body such as your sex organs?

Think of your eye—more wonderful than a camera. It sees color and motion, adjusts itself to dim light or bright sun, focuses automatically, never needs film, and develops its pictures instantly.

As we'll see in a later chapter, your sex organs are just as wonderfully made as your hand or your eye. For God Himself "arranged the parts in the body, every one of them, just as He wanted them to be" (1 Corinthians 12:18). Still we regard our sex organs differently than we regard body parts such as hands or eyes. Paul refers to sex organs as "unpresentable" parts that "are treated with special modesty" (1 Corinthians 12:23).

4
Is Sex a Secret?

A lot of people never talk about sex. Some think it's wrong to use the word. Many parents feel uncomfortable talking with their children about sex and reproduction. Whether such talk is easy or difficult in your home depends in part on the way your parents were raised. Those raised in homes where sex was a secret often have trouble talking about sex and sexuality even when they know they want to share their thoughts and feelings.

Perhaps you sense this hesitation in your home. You might be able to make the situation a little easier for your parents by asking some of the questions you have in a serious, mature way. You'll find most parents quite willing to talk once their first embarrassment has worn off.

Why might it be hard to talk about sex?

Try making a list of questions that you'd like to ask your parents, and find a time to ask them when nothing else is interfering. Don't dump all of your questions on your parents at once; try one, and see if that breaks the ice. You have a real chance to show your parents that you are growing up and want to talk to them in a mature way. It's a good way to improve communications in your family and to help the family grow together.

In what ways do people sometimes cheapen God's gift of sex?

Parents aren't the only ones you can get information from. You probably know another adult—a pastor, counselor, teacher, or relative—whom you like and who might be willing to listen to your questions. Sometimes friends can be helpful, but often they don't know any more about sex than you do. Even those friends who seem to talk most freely about sex may be giving you more imagination than facts, and you want facts.

Obviously there's a lot of talk about sex in school, but so much of it gives sex a bad name. Some people use slang terms, dirty jokes, and degrading laughter to cover their own embarrassment, lack of information, and misconceptions about sex. Such activity cheapens God's wonderful gift and increases the misunderstandings many young people have.

Our sex (or female gender) is a precious gift from God. It should be treated with great respect and discussed in ways that bring glory to God. After all, our bodies are "temples" of the Holy Spirit (1 Corinthians 6:19). It is important to have accurate, appropriate information about human sexuality. We don't want the temple of the Holy Spirit to be plundered through disrespect or inappropriate or wrongful use of any part of it. When you have questions about any aspect of your body, be sure to seek answers from those who share your faith in Jesus. Talk to a trusted adult who knows the answers to your questions, is willing to talk, treats sexual terminology and attitudes with respect, and thanks God for making you who and what you are.

5

You're Changing into a New You

You probably don't need the title of this chapter to know that its words are true. You probably knew something was different when your clothes didn't fit anymore. Or when you had trouble not tripping as you walked across a level floor. Or maybe when your moments of depression or frustration increased. No, you probably don't need a book to tell you that you're changing. You see it, feel it, and sense it all the time.

What are some things that adolescents worry about?

It's called **adolescence**, and it is the time of changing from a child into an adult. It is a very necessary trip, and often it will be exciting for you. But it also will be frustrating both to you and to others, mostly because of the changes happening in you and your concerns about them. Since joy and frustration are both part of adolescence, you might as well look forward to them and accept them.

Your body is changing and so is your personality. You feel more strongly about big things and little things. You want to be more involved in decisions. You want to be on your own to try out some new ideas, to do some new things. It's all part of growing up. At times, you'll feel pulled in both directions. Half the time you'll want the freedom of an adult, and half the time you'll want the security of a child. And there's not a lot you can do about it. Just try to accept it. You won't be the only one with feelings like these.

Why is it important for you to respect your body?

The best thing you can do is remember who you are. God made you, and He cares and provides for you at each stage of your growing from baby to girl to woman.

What do we know about God and His love even as we face changes in our own lives and in the lives of those around us?

Jesus, your Savior, promises always to love and forgive you and to guide and remain with you along life's path. Use adolescence as a time to discover who you are and to develop your own style, appreciate your personality, and respect the body you've been given. Be what you are—in Him!

As you work at finding out what and who you are, you're going to look around at others. You'll see some people who are what you want to be and many who aren't. Use these models to shape your actions, but don't lose yourself in the process. Heroes and role models are fine, but remember that you are you, and most of what you're going to be will come from inside you, not from anyone else.

It's so easy to assume that popularity depends on what you are, what you have, or how you look. But you'll find more often that it's based on how you treat, respect, and act toward others. Be yourself, without ever forgetting that others are important too. God has given you a lot. Your happiness will depend on how well you use those gifts and how comfortable you are with them.

Your Body Is Changing

Most of us have a time in our life when we grow very rapidly. This is called a **growth spurt**. You already may have begun a growth spurt. You may still be waiting. You don't need to worry if it hasn't hit you yet—it will. You'll almost be able to see your legs stretch out. You'll outgrow your clothes before you wear them out.

Most girls enter this stage between 9 and 12; boys usually enter it later, most often between 12 and 14. It's not at all unusual for girls to be taller than boys during the junior high years. It might be a little embarrassing or awkward that this happens just when boys and girls start noticing each other, but usually by age 15, boys catch up and grow taller than most girls.

You'll become much more aware of your height and weight during these years. You'll measure, weigh, and compare with others frequently, and you'll probably be concerned when you don't seem to be growing as fast as others or when others aren't growing as fast as you are. Differences in growth rate are common—and normal.

Few girls are exactly the size they'd like to be. Some are larger than their mothers, but not all. You may be the tallest in your class, or the shortest. You may be heavier or lighter than you would like. Most girls

will add 5 or 6 pounds a year by the time they're 15. Boys will gain 12–20 pounds a year at age 14 or 15, and after that maybe 6 or 8 pounds a year. Heredity has a lot to do with it, but so does what and how you eat.

The main thing to remember is that differences are normal—and good. Imagine a world where all of us matured at exactly the same rate and wound up exactly the same size and shape. What a bore! God knew what He was doing when He made each person unique. Not everyone is cut out to be an interior decorator or a star athlete. Instead, you may excel as a musician, writer, computer whiz, or designer. There's a place for everyone and a role for everyone. Try them all until you find the one that fits best; then accept it, and do the best you can in that role.

One of the changes you'll be most concerned about is the way you look. Your face is changing just like the rest of your body. Your mouth, nose, and chin are all starting to look more like an adult's than like a child's. You'll see differences when you compare your grade-school pictures with what you see in the mirror.

And that mirror is going to concern you frequently. Sometimes you're not going to like the way your hair looks. And you're probably going to spend a lot of time trying to make it look like someone else's. That might work, at least until the first gust of wind. But your biggest concern in the mirror is sure to be your complexion.

You may go through a time when **acne**—blackheads or pimples or something more bothersome—will affect your complexion. You may have real problems with acne. If basic facial cleanliness and standard acne treatments don't seem to be controlling it, talk to your doctor about it. Acne is not a fun part of growing up, but people do understand it's a common condition. They probably won't notice it as much as you do. And the good news is that it usually lessens or passes by the time you are 18 or 19.

Growing Sexually

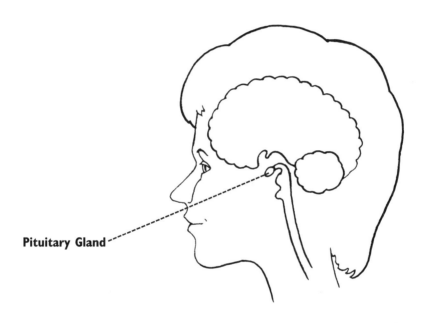

Pituitary Gland

The **pituitary gland**, located at the bottom of your brain, has been regulating most of the growth changes taking place in your body. This gland also has caused your sexual glands to mature. As that happens, growth usually slows down and sexual maturity is reached. These glands produce **hormones**, which cause a number of changes in your body. The most obvious of these changes are those that distinguish girls from boys.

You will notice that your hips become wider and your breasts begin to grow, perhaps as early as age 10 or 11. Hair will begin to grow under your arms, on your legs, and in your pubic area. Your voice will mature and become richer and fuller.

Boys generally experience the changes associated with puberty sometime between ages 12 and 17. A boy's chest will expand and his shoulders will become wider. Hair will appear under his arms, on his chest, on his face, and in his pubic area. His voice, too, will change, but not as easily as does a girl's.

Remember, these changes will occur at different times and in different ways. You may be maturing faster than most of your peers, or you may appear to be standing still. But you are changing, even if you can't see it or feel it yet.

Perhaps at times you feel embarrassed about the changes that are taking place in your body. But embarrassment can be healthy and good, a normal reaction that shows you are demonstrating proper regard for your body. God desires His followers to be concerned about issues of sexual purity and modesty. Remember that every adult has been through adolescence and has experienced what you are going through.

At times you're sure to get depressed about all the changes happening in and around you, and there will be moments when others just can't seem to understand your moods and feelings. Even when your friends and parents get impatient, God understands. He has a plan for you. His patience never grows thin; He's watching and He's in control. His love continues even when you and everyone else and the whole world are changing.

These thoughts and feelings are not unusual or abnormal. They are very much a part of growing up, a very natural part of learning to adjust to a growing body. Some of them show you need assurance; others show you need information. The chapters that follow in this book provide both. As you prepare to read and discuss them, you might find it helpful to review or to add to the questions you've already written down in chapter 1. You may want to share the questions with a close female friend or confidant who can relate to what you are experiencing, or you may wish to keep them for yourself as you read the following chapters.

Remember:

You may feel like a stranger to yourself. You may not be sure what is happening.

You may feel embarrassed talking to others, even those your own age, especially if they're developing at a different rate than you are.

You may feel out of place if you haven't developed as much as some of your friends have.

You might have trouble being honest about your own feelings, even with yourself.

You might feel pressure to conform to what others expect of you and to look and act like everyone else, even when you don't want to.

You might find yourself wanting to be alone more than ever before.

You might be trying to act more grown up than you really are.

You might find yourself thinking more about boys, even dreaming or fantasizing about sex. You might be feeling guilty about these thoughts and the feelings that go along with them.

And as you walk the journey through this stage, remember that

- God loves you; He made you just the way you are;
- you need to learn to respect yourself and your body before you can start respecting other people and their bodies; and
- your parents and other adults made it through adolescence, and so will you.

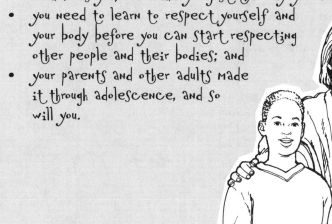

6

Becoming a Woman

You are experiencing or are about to experience a miracle called **puberty**—the time during adolescence when you are physically mature enough to become a mother. Those parts of your body that work together to make a baby are getting ready. If you have not already seen signs that the system is working, you soon will.

The physical indication that a girl has become a woman begins with the **ovaries**, the female organs of reproduction located near the center of the body. When the ovaries mature, they begin to develop egg cells smaller than a pinpoint. Once this happens, one egg cell or **ovum** is released from the ovaries about every 28 days. This is called **ovulation**.

From the ovaries, the tiny egg moves to the nearby **fallopian tube**, which leads to the **uterus** or womb. Fertilization occurs in the tube. The fertilized egg arrives in the uterus in about four days. In the uterus, the ovum—if it has been fertilized by a male cell—will grow to become a baby.

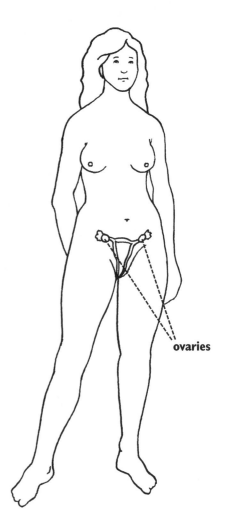

ovaries

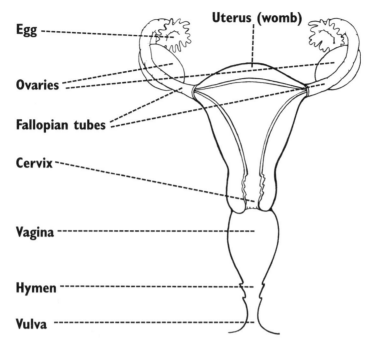

Egg

Ovaries

Fallopian tubes

Cervix

Uterus (womb)

Vagina

Hymen

Vulva

The uterus is a thick-walled, stretchy, hollow organ, about the size and shape of a fist. It can expand, like a balloon, to hold a growing baby. At the lower end of the uterus is the **cervix**. The cervix opens into the **vagina**, the passageway from the uterus to the outside of the body.

The outside opening of the vagina is between the legs, where it is covered by folds of skin called the **vulva**. At the top of the vulva, where the inner folds of skin meet, is the **clitoris**, a rounded tip of flesh the size of a pea.

The outside opening of the vagina in most girls is partially covered by the **hymen**, a thin membrane. This opening lies between two other openings in the woman's body. In front is the **urethra**, from which urine leaves the body, and in back is the **anus**, from which solid waste processed by the large intestine leaves the body.

Egg cells that leave the ovaries and are not fertilized soon break up and pass from the walls of the uterus through the vagina as a combination of waste tissue and blood. This occurs about two weeks after they leave the ovaries. The process is called **menstruation**. Most girls begin to menstruate when they are 12 or 13, but some begin to menstruate as early as 9 or as late as 16. Since the body has a regular period in which this occurs, menstruation is commonly called a woman's **period**. The normal period lasts from 3 to 7 days and occurs approximately every 28 days. The first periods are likely to be irregular and even skip a month or two before a regular cycle is established.

Menstruation is not a sickness; it is the regular reminder that your body is ready for motherhood when you, your husband, and God decide it is time for fertilization to occur.

Some discomfort may occur during menstruation, but most women feel okay and continue their normal schedules and routines during that time. If you do experience cramps in your lower abdomen or aching in the lower back, especially at the beginning of your period, and if the pain or discomfort seems unusual, talk to your parents or to your doctor about it.

To protect your clothing during menstruation, you may use sanitary pads available in various sizes and thicknesses. Or you may prefer tampons, little rolls of absorbent material that are inserted into the vagina. Consult your mother, a school nurse, or a doctor if you have any questions about which to use.

After the menstrual period is over, the process repeats itself. Another egg cell matures and is released about two weeks after menstruation, when the follicle (the larger cell mass sheltering the growing egg) ripens. If the egg is not fertilized, menstruation again occurs. The whole series of events is called the menstrual cycle and normally repeats itself, except during pregnancy, about every 28 days until a woman is 45 to 55 years old, when her ovaries no longer release egg cells.

Although questions about ovulation, fertilization, and menstruation are perhaps the most common that girls your age ask, you may have other questions about the development and maturing of your body. Perhaps you are concerned that your breasts don't seem to be developing as quickly or as fully as those of other girls your age or that they are developing too quickly or too fully. You may think it would be convenient if patterns were more consistent— that all girls' breasts started developing at exactly 11 years, for example—but that is not the way that God decided your body ought to work. You have your own personal growth pattern or clock. You can be sure that you will develop at just the rate God intends for your body. That may be earlier or later than some of your friends. It will happen, and it is normal to be different.

These are the signs that show you're maturing:

- Your hips start to broaden.
- Your breasts may begin developing (and it's not unusual for one breast to grow more rapidly than the other).
- Your pubic hair begins growing (this usually occurs before menstruation and will appear in many variations of shape and amount).
- You may notice a clear, whitish discharge from your vagina.
- You're growing quickly.

There you have it. The process may be awe-filled, but it is not awful. There is a big difference. God formed the first man from the dust of the ground, but the first woman He fashioned from one of Adam's ribs. Thus woman is a unique creation, created by a loving God for a different purpose than man—not to compete with him but to complement and complete him in society and especially within marriage.

Women and men are attracted to each other. They recognize and value the wholeness they experience when they are together, just as Adam did. (See Genesis 2:23.) Women who honor God recognize their responsibility to establish for themselves and encourage in other women standards of purity in dress, behavior, words, and choices. You are wonderfully made with a body capable of bearing new life. You have been given a wonderful gift, but with this gift comes the responsibility to treat it properly and to respect it.

When you become a woman, God's design is for you to be a blessing to the people He has placed into your life. Someday you may marry and be blessed with a relationship in which you love, encourage, and nurture your husband. You may bear a child, maybe many children, and have a special relationship in which you will have the opportunity to raise your children in a godly home where Christlike behaviors are both taught and lived.

What aspect of womanhood do you look forward to most?

Whether or not you marry or bear children doesn't change the gift or the wonder of God's plan for you as a woman. You are complete, special, important, and made in the image of God Himself. You are becoming a woman, someone who lives and breathes and loves and gives, someone who can join with the women of the Bible in celebrating your relationship with God, as in the words of Hannah, "My heart rejoices in the Lord" (1 Samuel 2:1).

7

About Boys and Men

Boys may be different from girls, but they have just as many questions. The questions are slightly different, but they show many similar concerns about sex. Boys may wonder
- What size should a penis be?
- Is it wrong to have "wet dreams"?
- What makes me feel the way I do about sex?

Questions like these are normal, natural, and necessary. When a boy reaches puberty, he becomes a man and is physically capable of being a father. There is even less consistency regarding when boys will reach puberty than there is with girls. One 14-year-old boy may not yet have any sign of hair on his face, while another the same age might be 6'2" tall and wearing a beard. A foot difference in height between boys this age is not at all unusual. Boys usually reach puberty between 13 and 16, a year or two after girls. This fact helps explain why girls are usually far more interested in dating during junior high than are boys. But the time will come when boys will catch up, and it will come soon.

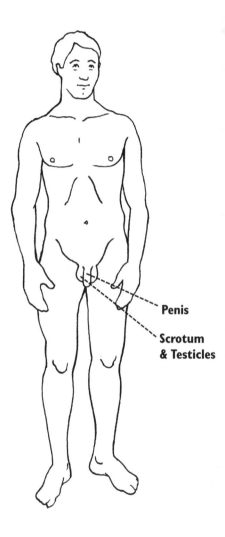

Penis

Scrotum & Testicles

Although a man's reproductive system is less complicated than a woman's and doesn't run by a calendar, it is no less miraculous and no less interesting. The two most important parts of the man's reproductive system are the **testicles** and the **penis**. The testicles produce **sperm**, the male cell that fertilizes the female egg. They also produce the hormone that causes boys' voices to become lower and hair to develop on their bodies at puberty. The two testicles hang behind the penis in a bag called the **scrotum**.

In order to produce sperm cells, the testicles must have a temperature that is a little lower than the temperature inside the body. The temperature must be kept constant, or the sperm cells already produced will die. How did God design the scrotum and testicles to take care of these needs?

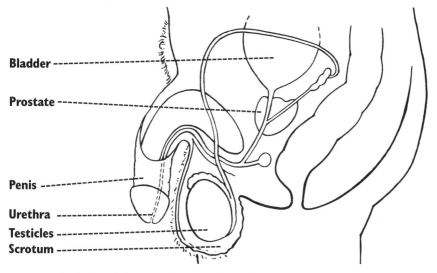

Bladder

Prostate

Penis

Urethra

Testicles

Scrotum

God placed the testicles outside the body. He designed the scrotum so it automatically contracts and draws the testicles closer to the body when the outside temperature grows colder. When the body overheats, the scrotum relaxes so the testicles may be farther from the warm pelvis. So the testicles do not injure each other when body movement brings the legs close together, God designed one testicle to hang lower in the scrotum than the other. What a miracle of God the scrotum and testicles are!

The penis hangs between the legs, in front of the testicles. It is made up of spongy tissue filled with large blood vessels. The average penis is three to four inches in length when it is limp, but penis size varies greatly from man to man. The size of the penis has nothing to do with a man's ability to have sexual intercourse or to become a father.

At birth, the end of the penis is partly covered by a loose skin called the **foreskin**. Some boys have this skin removed, usually just after birth, by a simple operation called **circumcision**. The reason for circumcision may be medical (the foreskin is too tight) or hygienic (some believe it is easier to keep a circumcised penis clean).

Through the center of the penis runs the **urethra**, the tube through which both sperm cells and urine leave the body. The urethra continues inside the body, extending to the bladder, where urine is stored.

If both sperm and urine pass through the urethra, do they come out at the same time? No. God has provided a wonderful mechanism to keep the sperm and urine separate. A valve at the upper end of the urethra opens to let the urine pass out. This same valve closes tight, keeping the urine in the bladder, when sperm pass through the urethra.

The sperm, then, move from each testicle, where they are produced, up through thin tubes inside the body. These tubes—one from each testicle—are connected with the **prostate gland** at the base of the bladder. The prostate gland produces a whitish fluid in which the sperm cells swim. The sperm cells and this fluid together are called **semen**.

An erection of the penis occurs when the blood vessels in the penis expand to bring more blood into the penis. Valves in the vessels keep this blood under pressure, causing the spongy walls of the penis to expand and become hard. Even babies and young boys experience **erections**, but they are more common after a boy reaches puberty.

Sometimes erections occur from physical reasons, such as the need to urinate. Even tight clothes can cause an erection. The most common cause, though, is sexual excitement. Movement of or pressure on the erect penis, such as happens during sexual intercourse, will eventually result in an **ejaculation**, the release of semen from the penis in a series of throbbing spurts. The amount of this white, sticky fluid is one to three teaspoons. Though sperm cells are only a small part of the fluid, one ejaculation can contain as many as 400 million sperm, each capable of fertilizing a single female egg.

Sometimes, at night, young men experience an ejaculation and wake up worried and upset. This is called a **nocturnal emission** or "wet dream," and it is perfectly normal. It is simply the body getting rid of excess semen. It first happens to most boys when they are 13 to 16 years old. Some young men have a lot of nocturnal emissions; some have few. The experience is natural and should not be thought of as abnormal or harmful.

How does a boy's body change during adolescence?

God has given each man a wonderful body. Like a woman, a man has the potential to start new life, although not every man will become a father. Of greater importance is how a man uses or controls the fact that he is a man in the relationships he builds with others. God made men as they are to be a blessing to others and to Him. It's a challenge and an opportunity to be a man. For men, part of living a life of love includes being spiritual leaders in society and in the home, where they have the responsibility to bring up children "in the training and instruction of the Lord" (Ephesians 6:4).

God's plan for man was damaged by the first sin of the first man—Adam. But we can all rejoice in God's plan for us through the Son of Man—Jesus, who is also the true God. Romans 5:19 says that "just as through the disobedience of the one man the many were made sinners, so also through the obedience of the one man the many will be made righteous." Jesus lived in perfect obedience to God's will, died to earn our forgiveness and salvation, and rose again as a demonstration of His victorious power. Jesus is a real male hero and the ultimate male role model. He sacrificed Himself to achieve our salvation. Through Word and Sacrament, He empowers His followers to "live a life of love, just as Christ loved us and gave Himself up for us as a fragrant offering and sacrifice to God" (Ephesians 5:2).

What does it mean to you that Jesus died to pay for your sins?

8

The Miracle of Birth

"So God created man in His own image, in the image of God He created him; male and female He created them. God blessed them and said to them, 'Be fruitful and increase in number; fill the earth and subdue it'" (Genesis 1:27–28a).

These words from Genesis show how God made man and woman for each other. He wanted them to be happy together, and He wanted them to use their bodies to produce the children that would someday fill the earth. For this reason He made men and women different, and He made those differences something that would cause men and the women to be attracted to each other. This sexual attraction is a gift of God. Men and women are made in a way and with feelings that cause them to want to be together.

As you grow older, you will feel this attraction more and more. You will want to be with boys—in groups or with one person. As you grow older, you will want to spend more time with boys. You may well begin to spend time with one special young man. As you get to know each other, you may fall in love and begin to look forward to marriage. Doing planned activities with a person of the other sex is called dating. Through dating, a man and a woman get to know each other. If a first date leads to a second or more dates, the two people usually enjoy being together and doing things together.

Some Christians encourage courting rather than dating. Courting refers to actions or activities undertaken in the effort to secure a mate. In the process of courting, couples develop romantic relationships only with those each would consider a potential spouse. Ideally, courting relationships grow out of friendships. The man and woman who have identified character qualities they desire in a godly mate allow their relationship to grow

What advantages may courtship have over dating in leading to a godly, satisfying marriage?

What qualities would you most desire in a spouse?

over time as they get to know each other and each other's families. Over time, they explore and share with each other their values and beliefs about God, finances, and free-time activities and make plans for the new life they will build together in marriage.

God's plan for a husband and wife to live together in a faithful commitment under His blessing and with His strength and guidance was first instituted by Him for Adam and Eve, predating the fall of humanity into sin. In marriage, a man and woman build a new life together through which they love and serve both God and each other. They work together to share God's love in their community and in the world. God passes the knowledge of His grace and goodness from one generation to the next within the family the married couple builds together. When a man and woman live together outside the commitment of marriage, on a temporary or trial basis, they are showing disregard for God's will.

Marriage is God's plan for establishing families. Part of God's design for marriage is to provide babies with mothers and fathers who will love them and care for them. Because of the special and unique relationship husband and wife enjoy in marriage, God wants only married people to engage in the close, intimate, and loving act known as **sexual intercourse**. "For this reason a man will leave his father and mother [the family where he grew up] and be united to his wife, and they will become one flesh" (Genesis 2:24). When a man and woman marry, they begin a new family, in which they can, with the blessing of God, give birth to children and love and care for them.

Sexual intercourse is a very special part of marriage. It's a unique way for a husband and wife to show their love for each other. When a husband and wife are feeling close and loving, they find a private place to be together—usually their bedroom. They kiss and caress each other. Gradually they become ready for intercourse. In sexual intercourse, the husband's erect penis is put into the wife's moist vagina. The penis ejaculates semen into the wife's vagina. Both the husband and wife usually feel pleasure during sexual intercourse and feel relaxed and satisfied afterwards. Soon after ejaculation, the penis again becomes limp.

If the woman has recently produced an egg cell, she can become pregnant. The man's sperm meet the egg cell. When one sperm enters the egg cell, that cell becomes fertilized— that is, no other sperm cell can now enter it,

What happens when an egg cell becomes fertilized?

and that fertilized cell is the beginning of a new human being. This means the married couple have **conceived** a child. The fertilized egg gradually moves into the uterus, attaches itself to the wall of the uterus, and begins to grow. At this moment it is smaller than a pinpoint. Until the end of the second month, it is called an **embryo**. After that, until the baby is born, the growing child is called a **fetus**, which in Latin means "young one."

Since extra blood is needed to nourish the growing egg as it develops into a baby, ovulation and menstruation do not occur while a woman is pregnant. The missing of a period is one way a woman senses she might be pregnant and is a reason for her to visit her doctor for an examination or tests that will make sure. If the woman is pregnant, the doctor will instruct her on the best way to care for her body in order to give her baby the best chance to develop normally.

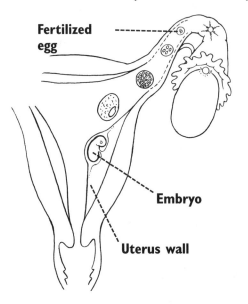

Fertilized egg

Embryo

Uterus wall

About nine months after the egg and the sperm joined, the baby will be ready to be born. For several months, the mother and father are able to feel their baby move in the mother's womb. Shortly before birth, the fetus usually turns in such a way that its head is pointed downward in the uterus. Then the muscles of the uterus, which have stretched to make room for the growing baby, begin to tighten and push, forcing the baby from the uterus into the vagina.

When this process called **labor** begins, the mother knows the birth will come soon and usually goes to the hospital so a doctor can help with the delivery. The baby usually arrives in the world headfirst from the vagina and soon gives out its first cry, a sign that it is breathing on its own. The **umbilical cord**, which joined the mother and baby in the womb and through which the baby received all its nourishment for nine months, is cut, leaving the **navel** or belly button on the baby's stomach.

Following the baby's birth, the **placenta** leaves the mother's body through the vagina. The placenta is the mass of blood vessels that grew in the uterus to help provide nourishment for the baby. God's miracle of conception and birth is now complete.

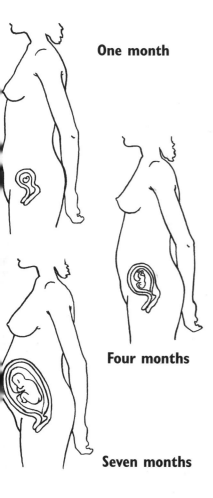

One month

Four months

Seven months

After the baby is born, the mother's uterus, vagina, and vulva slowly return to their normal size. If the mother breast-feeds her new baby, her breasts grow larger and begin to produce milk. If she chooses to bottle-feed her child, her breasts stop producing milk and return to their normal size.

Sometimes the embryo or fetus does not develop normally because of disease, injury, or some other problem. When this occurs and the baby is unable to survive or develop properly in the mother's uterus, her body rejects the dead fetus and pushes it from the body in a process called a **miscarriage**. It is estimated that about 15 percent of known pregnancies (the mother is aware that she is pregnant) end in miscarriage and that 30 to 50 percent of fertilized eggs are miscarried before the mother even knows she is pregnant. The process God designed to get you from a fertilized egg to the person you are today is an amazing miracle.

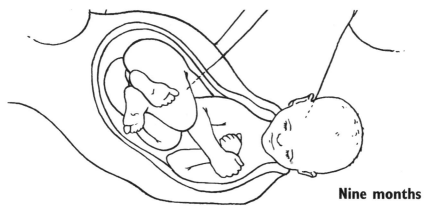

Nine months

"The Baby Looks Just Like You!"

Who in your family do you look like? Maybe you have your father's eyes or your mother's hair texture. Maybe you don't look very much like either of them. Maybe you are adopted, and you don't know which birth parent you look like. Regardless, both your father and your mother passed on to you a number of the features you have.

The sperm cell from the father contains 23 tiny elements called chromosomes. Each chromosome contains hundreds of parts called genes, which determine what the child will look like. There are genes for the color of the skin, for the shape of the head, for body size—for all of the traits that describe how you look.

The egg cell of the mother also contains 23 chromosomes, each with hundreds of genes. When the father's sperm cell unites with, or **fertilizes**, the mother's **ovum** or egg cell, the fertilized cell has 46 chromosomes that determine what the new baby will look like—half of them from the mother and half from the father. Each of the father's 23 chromosomes is matched or fitted with the same chromosome of the mother. The genes, which are the actual carriers of the features, may be either **dominant** or **recessive**. Dominant genes are stronger than recessive ones, which helps explain why parents can have children with different colored hair and eyes than they do.

Why do members of a family sometimes resemble each other?

Remember, too, that both the mother and father received their chromosomes from their parents, and they from their parents. So each newborn baby receives a good mix of characteristics from many different ancestors. That's why you may have brown eyes like your grandfather, rather than blue eyes like your mother or gray eyes like your dad.

What decided whether you're a boy or a girl? The sperm cell of the father. There are two kinds of sperm cells. One kind has what is called an X chromosome; the other has a Y chromosome. If a sperm with an X chromosome fertilizes the ovum, the baby will be a girl. If a sperm with a Y chromosome fertilizes the egg cell, the baby will be a boy.

The more we study the wonders of conception and birth, the more we will agree with the psalm: "I am . . . wonderfully made" (Psalm 139:14a)!

How does God involve men and women in His wonderful work of creation?

9
MeN and WomeN Are DiffereNt, AreN't They?

Sure, women and men are different. Recent studies by psychologists show that there are differences even between very young girl babies and boy babies. For example, girl babies respond sooner than boy babies to the voices and faces of their parents. Boy babies are more likely to scan the whole room and notice nearby objects. On average, adult women see better than men at night, but men see better during the day. But these and many other differences are average differences. They won't predict whether a certain woman or man can see better in daytime. Nor are the inborn differences between the genders very great.

As girls grow into women and boys grow into men, they are expected to have the characteristics usually associated with that gender. The trouble is, when we say all men and all women are or have to be a certain way, we may keep some individuals from using the good gifts and talents God has given them. For example:

In what ways are men and women the same? In what ways are they different?

- Karen is a 14-year-old super athlete but is having trouble getting on a baseball team.
- Jose enjoys cooking, but his brother says it's a "girl's job."
- Latoya loves to work on her dad's car. Some neighbors don't think that hobby is very "ladylike."

God created women and men to be different, but the differences were designed to bring them together, not to separate them. Because women and men were created to complement one another, females and males relate with others, communicate, and love differently. Generally, women are more verbal than men and build relationships as they connect on an emotional level. Men are more likely to communicate and build relationships around actions and activities.

Describe God's will for young men and women.

The most obvious differences between women and men are physical. But the physical differences were not meant to set a limit on things that are not physical. A woman might not be able to lift or carry as much weight as most men, but that doesn't mean she can't drive a moving van or manage a moving company as well as or better than many men. A man might not have spent as much time in a kitchen as a woman while they were growing up, but that doesn't mean he can't wash the dishes, do the laundry, or plan and prepare a seven-course dinner.

God has given all people gifts of all kinds to use in His service and in the service of others. The question is, what gifts has God given you—and how will you use them in a way that is respectful of God's plan for womanhood?

In a letter to Timothy, the apostle Paul describes God's will regarding the behavior of young women. Women are to "dress modestly, with decency and propriety, not with braided hair or gold or pearls or expensive clothes, but with good deeds, appropriate for women who profess to worship God" (1 Timothy 2:9–10). When we teach and interact with others, God's Word commands us, "Don't let anyone look down on you because you are young, but set an example for the believers in speech, in life, in love, in faith and in purity" (1 Timothy 4:12).

You will be deciding in the next few years how you want to spend your life. Be yourself! Honestly examine your interests and your abilities in light of God's will for you as His child. Ask God's Spirit for the power and ability to live your life for Him who died for you and rose again. Be proud that you are a woman, and look for ways to use what you are as fully as God intended in a way that gives credit to Him, to your sex, and to you. That was God's idea. Now take it and use it!

As God's children through faith in Christ Jesus, we are called to respect and appreciate the differences between men and women. At the same time, we are to respect and appreciate the similarities and never demonstrate demeaning, diminishing, or degrading attitudes toward one another.

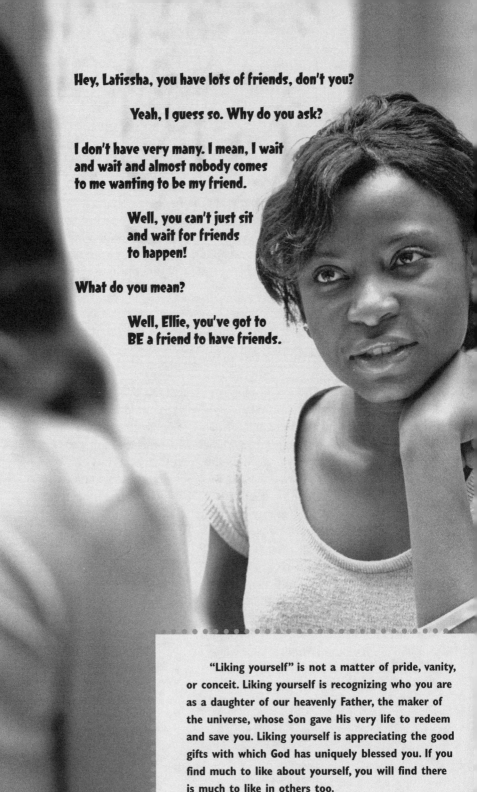

Hey, Latissha, you have lots of friends, don't you?

Yeah, I guess so. Why do you ask?

I don't have very many. I mean, I wait and wait and almost nobody comes to me wanting to be my friend.

Well, you can't just sit and wait for friends to happen!

What do you mean?

Well, Ellie, you've got to BE a friend to have friends.

"Liking yourself" is not a matter of pride, vanity, or conceit. Liking yourself is recognizing who you are as a daughter of our heavenly Father, the maker of the universe, whose Son gave His very life to redeem and save you. Liking yourself is appreciating the good gifts with which God has uniquely blessed you. If you find much to like about yourself, you will find there is much to like in others too.

10
Getting Along with Friends

Almost everyone wants to be with other people, to be liked, to be needed, to be included in groups and clubs and teams. And that's God's plan. He made people to live with and to share with other people. That's what the Church is—God's people living with and helping and loving one another.

If you marry someday, you will have a special person to live with and to relate to, and sex will be an important part of that relationship. But another part of being a woman is having friendships—close relationships with others—where sex is not a part.

You and Your Friends

Being a friend and having friends is a very important part of life. Especially during your teenage years, it is important to like yourself and to be with others who like themselves. If you don't like yourself, it's pretty hard for you to really like others and for them to think much of you. Even Jesus said to "love your neighbor as [you love] yourself" (Mark 12:31a). After all, who wants to be around people who can't do anything but run themselves down? Liking yourself, then, is part of being a good friend.

What makes a person a friend?

What else makes a person a good friend? Place checkmarks in the appropriate places on the following chart as you think about friendship and being a good friend.

A Friend...	I want a friend who	I see myself as a friend who
is understanding	___	___
listens	___	___
is pleasant to be around	___	___
can be trusted	___	___
can be counted on	___	___
is open	___	___
is helpful	___	___
respects the interests of other friends	___	___
is considerate	___	___
is courteous	___	___
has a good sense of humor	___	___
has good manners	___	___
is easy to talk to	___	___

Why are Christian friends special gifts from God?

Are there other things you'd add to your list? Are some of these things unimportant to you? One way to check out how friendly you are and a way to work at becoming more friendly is to use this list to examine yourself and to practice doing some of those things that you might not have been doing in your relationships with others. Being friendly to others will always be one of the best ways to get and to keep friends.

Friendships are helpful in developing the values that guide what you do. You may notice that some of the things you do are modeled directly after actions of your friends. Perhaps you feel that you have to talk like your friends, dress in similar ways, and do the same kinds of things. This is called **peer pressure**, or pressure from those your age, and it will be an important force in your life. No one wants to be too different; looking like your friends and doing what they do is an important part of feeling accepted and belonging to a group. On the outside, you want to look, dress, and act like everyone else. But on the inside are the goals, attitudes, beliefs, and values that make up the real you. Maturity results from struggling with the influence of these two forces until they match.

Most of the time it is okay to try to be like your friends, especially if your friends hold values and moral standards similar to yours. If you feel the constant pull from your friends to do things or say things that are different from the things that you believe are right, you are likely to create tension for yourself and for your relationship with your family.

What makes Jesus your best and truest friend?

Your best and truest friend is Jesus Himself. He knows your every thought, worry, fear, hope, and aspiration. He gave His very life to earn forgiveness for all the wrong things you have done and to grant you a home someday in heaven. Friends who share your love for Jesus are special gifts from God. They support and encourage you to live according to God's Word and to share the Good News of Jesus with others.

You should not avoid contact with those people who live differently than you. Instead, you can be a Christian example for them. You can share the Good News of God's love and forgiveness even with those who laugh at you for being a Christian. So look for ways to reach out and broaden your circle of friends. Too close an association with too small a group of friends is likely to stunt the growth of your personality.

At least you can make an effort to be friendly to everybody. A happy smile, a cheerful "hi"—even to strangers—can go a long way in helping people see you as a friendly person. It's pretty hard for anyone to ignore that kind of greeting, and it's a good way to get others to want to find out more about you.

What about Dating?

Even if you've never had a date, you've probably thought about dating. In the years ahead, the pressure to date and to talk about dating are going to increase. So even if you're not particularly excited about dating, it won't hurt to think about it and to talk about the reasons teenagers want to date. These are some of the more common reasons:

1. You don't want to be alone.
2. You need to feel accepted and worthwhile.
3. Some of your friends are dating.
4. You need to feel independent, to move away from family influence and be on your own.
5. You want a chance to try out adult behavior.
6. You want to develop close relationships with those of the other sex.
7. You want the special feeling that comes when someone cares enough for you to want to be with you.

No doubt you can add other reasons for wanting to date, but maybe your present thoughts about dating are more in the form of questions. Maybe you have some questions like these:

1. How old should I be before I start dating? Is it wrong not to want to date yet?
2. How can I show my affection toward a boy on a date without giving him the wrong idea?
3. Is it okay for me to ask a boy out? How do I get a boy to ask me out?
4. What do I do on a date?
5. What commitment am I making to the boy I go with on a date? What expectations will the boy I date have of me?

All of these are good questions, very normal ones for people your age. And when you ask them, you are going to find that lots of people have answers for you. You will have some of your own answers, your friends will have some answers, and your parents and other adults are bound to want to get a few of their answers in too.

Why might your parents have different ideas about dating than you do?

It's possible that your parents' answers will be different from your own. And that could cause conflict. Your parents will probably have some set ideas about dating—even rules or at least guidelines for dating. That's because they want the best for you.

It may not seem like it at the time, but they're really thinking of you and your interests. God holds them responsible for bringing you up as a loving, responsible Christian person. And He calls on you to love, honor, and respect them. The best way to handle the conflicts that arise is to talk openly about differences without arguing. Perhaps if you accept their rules without arguing, adjustments can be made as time goes on to allow for the maturity you've shown.

> **What is the purpose of dating? How can you witness to your faith during your dating years?**

Saying to your parents "everyone else can" may be true, but it probably won't help. It might be more successful to ask for special permission to stay out late for a special occasion than to push for blanket approval of a time they aren't comfortable with. Each situation will be different, though, and the best way always is to work with your parents in understanding and love.

The answers to most of the questions about dating can't be answered in some simple, standard way for everyone. God made you different from your friends, and your development will be different from theirs in many ways. You don't have to be like everyone else in the way you feel about dating, when you start dating, or even in what you do on a date.

Keeping that in mind, here are some answers to our earlier questions that can serve as guidelines as you and your parents come up with answers that work for you.

1. *How old should I be before I start dating? Is it wrong not to want to date yet?* There's no rule about when to start dating. You don't have to prove anything to anyone by dating if you don't feel like it. But you'll want to spend time with larger groups of people, both girls and boys, doing things you like to do. Show your interest in others and in their activities. Let your own interests grow. And if special interests develop in one or more boys, fine. Participating in planned activities involving peers of both genders is fine at any age. These activities may include a party, a school social, a volleyball game at the beach, a softball game in the park, or the like. No one is paired off with another specific person in this type of date—but girls and boys are getting to know one another better.

As you get to know what interests Jerome or John through a date with a group, you will be preparing yourself for a special kind of group date: Two or three boys ask two or three girls to a party at school, church, or in the neighborhood. This kind of "double dating," in turn, will help you feel more confident and will prepare you for single dating later.

Discuss with your parents whether you're ready yet for double dating—and discuss single dating too, which most young people don't begin until the high school years.

2. *How can I show my affection toward a boy on a date without giving him the wrong idea?* Read what we say in chapter 12, under "Sexual Experimentation." Avoid trying to see what you can get out of your date. Such an approach is selfish and self-centered. It conveys little respect for your date. Disrespecting another person also disrespects God and His will for His people. Avoid situations that increase temptations. Pray for God's Spirit to guide you. Remember God's command—and the good reasons He has for restricting sexual intercourse to marriage. Remember how much Christ loves you and your date—and that He gave Himself up for you on the cross!

3. *Is it okay for me to ask a boy out? How do I get a boy to ask me out?* If your parents approve of a boy/girl party and will be on hand to chaperone, invite the boy you're interested in. Or you may simply want to invite him to a social event you think he might enjoy. Be sure to ask early. And give him all the facts: when, where, and what the event is all about.

If you want a boy to ask you out, be friendly to him whenever you see him. Show you're interested in him. Whenever you see him, encourage him to talk about his activities—hobbies, schoolwork, athletic events. Try not to be too pushy. Many people shy away from others who try to take charge or who quite obviously hint that they want to be asked out.

4. *What do I do on a date?* Even when you're ready to date and want to, it's not always easy to start. You're nervous about accepting, or you're nervous about asking. You want to say and do just the right thing. Be yourself. You are a unique person whom God made and loves. Don't try to overdo the date but settle for the easy things—a movie, a trip to the mall, a party of some kind. Being with another couple or two or in a group lessens the chance for awkward times when you don't know what to say and reduces the temptation to go past the boundaries of proper action that you have set.

5. *What commitment am I making to the boy I go with on a date? What expectations will the boy I date have of me?* Remember the purpose of dating is to help you get to know and relate to boys. Whether the date is with a group or with just one boy, remember to respect yourself and all others as persons for whom Jesus died. Because you are God's child, through faith you can evidence His presence in your life in the words you speak and the things you do. Going with a boy on a date does not obligate you to any other commitments involving him. Some Christian young people make a list of qualities they desire in a future spouse and focus on dating only people with those qualities.

As you grow to be a woman, there will be times of doubt and disappointment, times of frustration, and maybe even times bordering on despair. But the dating years are great years during which you become the person you will be for a long time. God had a good reason for making the years of physical growth and the years of social growth happen at the same time. When they're finished, you'll feel ready to be an adult. They won't last all that long; enjoy them right now!

46

11
Getting Along with Family

You may have noticed that the amount of disagreement between you and others in your family has increased in the last couple of years. Such conflict certainly isn't pleasant, but it might help to realize that it's pretty common in most families. It doesn't automatically mean that your home is falling apart and that everyone is failing in their efforts to be a family. It probably does mean that both parents and children are adjusting to new roles. If everyone sees that it is part of development, these moments of conflict can teach both parents and children to understand and to better handle these new roles.

This process can be difficult. You've already read about the problems that arise about matters of sex, about growing up, and about dating. And you surely can think of other areas where you or your friends have run into trouble with parents. Whether you consider the things you argue about big things or little things, one of the biggest causes of misunderstanding is the unwillingness of either side to really listen to what the other is saying. Parent and child feel so strongly about their position that they don't consider the possibility of another point of view.

Why should parents and children take time to listen to one another?

Taking time to listen to the other person will help, and so will stopping to ask why you're getting so upset. Is it really worth it? Why is it so important to you and to the other person? Instead of trying to decide who is right and who is wrong, base your discussions in love and understanding.

Obviously you're never going to be able to do everything your parents expect you to, even if you wanted to. And they'll disappoint you, too, in the way they talk or act. But God's plan for the members of your family is that each of you is willing to forgive and share and grow and learn together in love.

How is your family God's gift to you? How does the world's definition of family differ from God's?

Sometimes parents really don't understand that you are capable of handling more responsibility; sometimes they simply expect too much. And perhaps you sometimes forget that your parents do most of what they do because they love you and want only what is best for you. It can be hard for parents to let go of the child whom they have raised and cared for in both good and bad times. Sometimes your growing up only means to them that they are growing old. Both sides can learn a lot about patience, understanding, and sharing the love and forgiveness that God's love makes possible. His presence during all arguments can take away a lot of the sting.

All this understanding won't take away the areas of conflict. They will still be there. Parents may continue to remind you what they did or didn't have when they were young. They may try to shape you into something they wanted to be but didn't get to be. Maybe they'll push you toward a profession they like but in which you have no interest.

And parents will continue to want a voice in your selection of friends—of either sex. But if you listen and try to understand what they are saying, you just may hear a little wisdom and a lot of love and understanding tucked around those words that seem to criticize everything you do. And sometimes, they might even be right!

You may be growing up in a single-parent home. The number of such homes is increasing and brings special needs and opportunities for teenagers. Managing such homes is especially hard for single parents, and they may expect you to carry more of the load and perhaps to grow up faster than you would need to in a two-parent home. At times, you may experience feelings of insecurity as you wonder where exactly you fit within the changing configuration of your family. It's not easy, but it's the kind of situation in which God has promised to supply a special measure of His Spirit.

What difference can God's love and forgiveness make in day-to-day family life?

Whatever your home environment, whether you live with one parent, two parents, or foster parents and whether you have younger brothers and sisters who torment you or older brothers and sisters to whom you constantly get compared, your family is God's gift to you, and you are God's gift to it.

You'll have times when you'd like to give your family back, and probably there will be times when they'd like to give you back. But your family is God's plan, His design, and He is right there watching and helping those who invite Him into their family. It's an awfully good idea to send that invitation, especially at the time when the argument starts and before those words and actions occur that you'll wish later you could take back. He'll be there immediately.

12
Special Questions

The subject of sex raises many questions that aren't always easy to talk about or to answer. This section will touch on some of the better-known problem subjects. If your own question isn't answered in this section, be sure to ask a trusted Christian adult: your parents, your pastor, your teacher, or your guidance counselor.

Pornography

One of the growing forms of temptation that you will have to face is **pornography**: pictures and writing that make sex dirty and sinful. Some Internet Web sites, magazines, immoral pictures, and X-rated movies show the body as something to be used, abused, and lusted after rather than something to be thankful for, admired, and treated as a gift of God. Most of these books, pictures, and places claim to be off-limits to those under 18 or 19 years of age. But junior high students may still come into contact with pornography—even though they may not be looking for it. We live in a society that glamorizes sex and bodies through ads, books, movies, TV, and the Internet. It's all around us.

It will not be an easy temptation for you to ignore, but there are things you can do. You can remember always that your body and the bodies of others are the gifts of God. You can be aware that such pornographic materials exist, yet you can avoid them. You can avoid those situations that might pull you into groups whose actions and words degrade sex and the human body. You can seek the support and encouragement of other young people who share your love of Jesus and desire to live for Him. You can pray daily for strength to resist the pressure to conform. (See Romans 12:2.) And you can take care not to tell improper stories regarding sexually explicit acts or to wear revealing clothing that may tempt others to think impure thoughts.

Masturbation

Masturbation is the handling or rubbing of the clitoris or penis to gain pleasure or until release of sexual pressure, or **orgasm**, is reached. In years past, parents, teachers, and books told teenagers that masturbation would lead to blindness, to deafness, to loss of hair, and even to **sterility** (the inability to have children) or insanity. None of these are true. Medical authorities agree that there are no harmful physical effects caused by masturbation.

Some authorities are concerned, though, that masturbation can turn into a kind of preoccupation of "self-love" that keeps young people from developing normal social relationships with others. While masturbating, a person often has thoughts that may later make her feel ashamed or guilty. These harmful effects of masturbation can't be ignored.

Here are some ways to overcome the habit of masturbation: spend more time in activities with others—sports, clubs, hobbies—whatever interests you and will bring you into contact with people. Avoid pictures and books and conversations that are sexually stimulating. "Whatever is true . . . whatever is pure, whatever is lovely . . . think about such things," writes the apostle Paul (Philippians 4:8). In other words, think about all the exciting, interesting, beautiful things and people in God's world. Most of all, ask God for His strength and power to resist temptation. And remember that He keeps on loving you and forgiving you for Jesus' sake.

Sexual Experimentation

Maybe you've heard friends brag about experiences with sex that no one else in the group has had. For many, these stories are like a game or contest. Each person wants to show she knows more or is more mature and sophisticated than anyone else in the group. Of course, these stories often are exaggerations—or even plain lies. But they can lead you to feel inferior, abnormal, or at least different from your friends. They can cause you to experiment with sex to prove yourself.

Certainly as you begin to date, you will find that you want to kiss, to hold, and to touch the boy you are with. Such activities are not wrong, but you will soon discover the need to draw some lines in your own mind about what is right.

To do something just to see if you can get away with it or to see how far you can go degrades the person you are with. It can't lead to friendship or to real love. If you want to do something to prove your courage or so you can brag about it, you are doing wrong.

Some young people engage in oral sex, the stimulation of another's sex organs by mouth, believing that they are not engaging in sex because they are not having sexual intercourse. But oral sex and other activities of a sexual nature that invade or substitute for the type of sexual intimacy reserved for a man and woman within marriage offends God's Law regarding sexual purity.

The best guideline seems to be drawing the line at those touches that might lead you and your partner beyond the point of control and into sexual intercourse. If you avoid situations that increase the chances of stepping beyond the line you have drawn, you will better enjoy your relationship. You will respect yourself and the person you are with. For example, don't get together in a house where no adults are home. Most teen pregnancies begin in someone's home.

Most of all, remember that as a Christian you can call on the power of God's Spirit. "Live by the Spirit, and you will not gratify the desires of the sinful nature. . . . The acts of the sinful nature are obvious: sexual immorality, impurity . . . and the like. . . . But the fruit of the Spirit is love, joy, . . . and self-control. . . . Since we live by the Spirit, let us keep in step with the Spirit" (Galatians 5:16, 19, 22, 23, 25).

Recreational Sex?

Popular culture and the entertainment industry would have us accept the notion that sexual intercourse outside of marriage is a normal, healthy, even expected aspect of adulthood. In addition to the influences of the world around us, the devil would have us go along with this perspective, which also appeals to our natural inclinations because they are contaminated by sin. These forces—the world, the devil, and our sinful nature—that work so mightily to lead us into sexual sin and its consequences—are sometimes referred to as the unholy trinity. 1 Corinthians 6:18–20 directs, "Flee from sexual immorality. All other sins a man commits are outside his body, but he who sins sexually sins against his own body. Do you not know that your body is a temple of the Holy Spirit, who is in you, whom you have received from God? You are not your own; you were bought at a price. Therefore honor God with your body."

Sexual immorality, which includes intercourse outside of marriage and all misuses of God's gift of sex, disobeys the will of our Father in heaven, who desires only what is best for us. And it does have harmful consequences. Taking part in intimate sexual activity outside of marriage negatively influences your attitude toward yourself and others. As St. Paul says, "He who sins sexually sins against his own body" (1 Corinthians 6:18b).

Why is sexual intercourse sinful before marriage but good and even commanded within marriage? Because God planned intercourse as the highest expression of love between a husband and a wife. Sexual intercourse in marriage unites a husband and wife into "one flesh." Misuses of God's gift of sex negatively influence how we think of and treat others as well as how we think of and regard ourselves.

The Bible warns against fornication and adultery. **Fornication** is sexual intercourse between unmarried people. **Adultery** is sexual intercourse by a married person with someone other than his or her spouse. In both of these sins, the man or woman gives in to his or her own selfish desires and disregards God's Law. By remaining a **virgin** until you are married, you are following God's Law and staying open to all the blessings He wants to give you.

Many people who give in to these sins, of course, claim that they can love the person they are having intercourse with even though they are not married to that person. But what kind of love is it that says, "My pleasure comes first. I don't care what God says or what may happen if I hurt my husband by having intercourse with someone else"? That is not love, it is lust.

When Jesus spoke in Matthew 5:28 about a "lustful" look and "adultery" in the heart, He wasn't talking about our good, God-created interest in and attraction to people of the other sex. He meant the selfish misuse of that desire. Love cares about and for the other person. Lust uses the other person for its own pleasure.

"Husbands, love your wives, just as Christ loved the church and gave Himself up for her" (Ephesians 5:25). Remember how Christ loves you! That's the way husbands, wives, and young people who are about to date can turn from lust and grow in love.

Birth Control

What is birth control? Any method that people who are having intercourse use to prevent pregnancy. There are a number of birth control methods. **Birth control pills** taken regularly by a woman prevent ovulation by making the body "think" pregnancy has taken place. **Birth control foam** used by a woman kills the sperm before they reach the egg. The **diaphragm** is a cap that a woman inserts into her vagina to keep the sperm from getting into her uterus.

In natural methods of family planning, a woman closely keeps track of her monthly periods, avoiding intercourse during those times each month when she is most likely to get pregnant. This method is called the **rhythm method**.

The most common form of birth control for males involves the use of a condom. **Condoms** fit over the penis and prevent the sperm from entering the vagina. Men and women also may be **sterilized** by having an operation that prevents pregnancy. On the man, this is done by cutting the tubes that carry sperm from the testicles. On the woman, it's done by tying shut the fallopian tubes. Both of these sterilization operations are usually permanent. They do not, however, affect the ability to have sexual intercourse.

Many Christians are concerned about the motives for practicing birth control, particularly if the couple does not want children and the responsibilities that children bring. Also, some Christian churches permit only "natural methods" of birth control since they view other methods as being against God's will.

Birth control allows a married couple to plan more carefully when to have children and how many they will have. Because birth control methods are readily available and to a certain extent remove the fear of pregnancy, they have no doubt encouraged more unmarried people to have intercourse. But in recent years there have been more unmarried pregnancies than ever before. Why is that? Well, for one, many unmarried people simply don't bother to use any birth control methods. Then, too, none of the birth control methods are 100-percent effective. Abstinence is the only birth control method that is 100-percent effective.

Abstinence means reserving intimate sexual activity for marriage. Since God's Word forbids intimate sexual activity outside of marriage, obedience to God involves waiting until marriage for sexual intimacy. Waiting is especially difficult when social and entertainment influences lean with so much pressure upon young people to conform. But God does not leave us alone to face these struggles and temptations. He strengthens and encourages us through His Word, offering to us the same power that enabled Joseph to abstain and resist the seductive pleadings of Potiphar's wife. (See Genesis 39:1–23.)

Unmarried—and Pregnant

There are more birth control devices than ever before, and people can get them more easily than ever before. Yet more unmarried girls are getting pregnant—even those from strong Christian homes. Very likely, you know of girls and boys who are experiencing or who have experienced this very real problem. And it is a problem in which both girls and boys are equally involved, because it takes a boy to get a girl pregnant.

The young girl who becomes pregnant faces several decisions about what to do. She and the father of the child may decide to marry. If they do, they need to be aware of the difficulties they will face. For example, such a marriage has four times as great a chance of ending in divorce as do other marriages. And such a marriage can interrupt or stop the couple from finishing school and developing their abilities. Nevertheless, such a marriage can succeed if both father and mother are willing to make the necessary sacrifices. As they trust in God for forgiveness and for strength, they can grow in their love for one another.

The girl also may decide to have the baby and to place it for adoption. Many girls choose to do this, letting the baby be placed in a home with parents who are able to provide for it and give it love and security. A mother who makes the sacrifice of giving up her child—and the child who is adopted by loving parents—will find special meaning in this word from God: "God sent forth his Son, born of woman, . . . so that we might receive adoption as sons. And because you are sons, God has sent the Spirit of his Son into our hearts, crying, 'Abba! Father!'" (Galatians 4:4–6 RSV).

Numerous unmarried women who are pregnant choose to have **abortions**—that is, to have the unborn embryo or fetus killed in their womb before it is born. But this is a terrible sin! Only God has the right to give and take away life. Killing an embryo or fetus is killing a human person.

Some girls decide to have the baby and to raise it, perhaps with the help of their parents and with the financial assistance of the child's father. Such a decision will cause problems, to be sure. The mother may find it hard to take care of her baby and also continue going to school. It may be more difficult for her to get married later. But again, this approach can work out as the mother looks to our Father in heaven for the support and strength she will need.

In any case, all those involved in an unplanned pregnancy need the strong support and forgiving love of relatives and friends. Most of them recognize their sin, and they need to hear God's forgiveness in Christ. They need help, too, to seek out God's will for their lives and for the baby who will be born. Regardless of the circumstances associated with any baby's birth, each individual is loved by God and redeemed by His Son.

Sexually Transmitted Diseases

What are **sexually transmitted diseases** (STDs)? STDs are diseases you get from having intercourse with—or sometimes from kissing—an infected person. There are many different and dangerous STDs. The most common are **chlamydia, herpes, syphilis, human papilloma virus** (HPV), and **gonorrhea**. Doctors are researching how to cure these diseases, yet more people are getting them. STDs infect millions of teenagers annually.

The chlamydia bacterium infects the urethra in men and women, and may inflame or scar the sex organs so the person becomes infertile. The herpes simplex virus (Type 2) causes itching and painful blisters on the **genitals**. Signs of syphilis first appear 10 to 90 days after infection as a *chancre* sore on or near the sex organs, but such sores don't always occur. HPV causes warts on both women's and men's genital organs and also cancer of the cervix. Symptoms are not always noticeable in gonorrhea, although infected men sometimes notice a whitish discharge from the penis 3 to 8 days after infection. Women usually have no early signs that they have gonorrhea, but the later effects of the disease are as serious for them as they are for men.

Many sexually transmitted diseases can be treated and cured by early diagnosis and medical treatment. But because the diseases may not give early warning signs, many people believe they don't have these diseases and so they let them go untreated. If they aren't treated, chlamydia, syphilis, HPV, and gonorrhea are extremely serious. They can lead to blindness, heart trouble, infertility, cancer, and even death. Although herpes is not life-threatening for most people, there is no cure. Genital warts can be treated, but there is no cure for HPV.

In 1981, doctors began to report a new disease called **AIDS**. AIDS is caused by a virus that can be passed from one person to another mostly by sexual contact or by sharing drug needles and syringes used for "shooting" drugs. The AIDS virus attacks a person's immune system and damages one's ability to fight other diseases. The body can then easily get all kinds of life-threatening diseases, such as pneumonia, meningitis, and cancer. There is no cure for AIDS and no vaccine to prevent it.

Many AIDS patients do not get the disease through sex. Some get it from infected, shared needles when shooting drugs. Others become infected through contaminated blood products. And some are born with it, because an infected mother can pass AIDS to her fetus, and later through her breast milk. Nevertheless, the great majority of AIDS patients get the disease from sexual contact. It can take up to 6 months to test positive for the HIV virus and then another 10–15 years for symptoms to appear.

Chlamydia, herpes, syphilis, HPV, and gonorrhea come mainly from sexual contact. To prevent them, refrain from intercourse outside of marriage and stay faithful within marriage. If you ever have any fear that you might have such a disease, see a doctor immediately.

Homosexuality

Homosexuality means sexual attraction to those of the same sex. **Homosexuals** include men who are attracted to men and women who are attracted to women. Often, a homosexual person is said to be gay. Women homosexuals also are called lesbians.

What makes some people homosexuals? No one knows for certain. But God's Word is clear that homosexual behavior is against God's will and is sinful.

You may never feel temptation toward any sort of sexual relationship with someone of your own sex. It's normal to admire and desire to be with someone of the same sex, such as a good friend or an older person. This is not homosexual behavior.

Remember, too, that no one can identify homosexuals by the way they look. Often people are called homosexual for reasons based on hatred, suspicion, and ignorance, certainly not on fact. Remember that Christ died and rose again for the forgiveness of homosexuals and heterosexuals alike. God says clearly what is wrong, and He says clearly that sin is forgiven in Christ. Both homosexuals and heterosexuals can be guilty of sinful lusts. But God calls all people to repentance—to admit and be sorry about sin, to receive the forgiveness Jesus offers, and to turn away from sin to lead a godly life through the power of the Holy Spirit at work in us. No one who asks for forgiveness is beyond receiving it fully. Only the love of God in Jesus and the power He brings can give you the strength to reject temptation and to reach out in forgiveness and Christian love.

Feeling Guilty

Young people sometimes do things connected with sex or think about sex in a way that they know is wrong. They feel guilty and know that they have fallen short of their own standards, God's standards, and the standards others expect them to follow. The result can be some pretty bad moments spent criticizing themselves for what they've thought or done.

Feeling guilty about sex comes from an awareness of failure to obey God's Law. These feelings serve a purpose just like guilty feelings about other things you do wrong. You say something nasty to your parents, you cheat on a test, you lie about something else, and you feel guilty. Sexual sins are no different from other sins in the eyes of God. They are wrong.

But the great thing about being a Christian is that God the Judge is also God the Lawyer on our behalf and the God of forgiveness. God the Father sent His Son to die for all your sins and all the sins of everybody else. With His resurrection came our forgiveness that wipes out all our sins and all our guilt about them. Feeling guilty makes you look for help. Thank God that Jesus brings help and forgiveness. Trust His Word to you: "Your sins are forgiven . . . go in peace" (Luke 7:48, 50).

Jesus also said, "Sin no more" (John 8:11 KJV). Well, you know you're going to sin again, but the forgiveness God gives also gives the power to live a new life, one aimed at living more the way God wants, growing in faith and growing in your faith life. It also gives the power to confess, to apologize, and to forgive others when they do things to you that are wrong. And, above all, it gives the assurance that whenever you fall short of your own goals for living—and you will—the same forgiveness is waiting every time, as fully and totally as the first time.

Sexual Abuse

Sexual abuse happens when a person asserts power and authority over another—usually a child—to obtain sexual pleasure. The abuser might be an older child or an adult. In a sexual abuse situation, the abuser might kiss the child in a sexual way, touch the child on the genitals, make the child touch him or her, or even have sexual intercourse with the child. Sexual abuse is always the fault of the abuser and never the fault of the child or the abused.

Most children will not be abused, but all children need to be careful. If someone says or does something that makes you feel uncomfortable, it's important to tell your parents or another adult you trust right away. Those who take sexual advantage of others are not normal, and they are committing a crime. They need treatment, and they need to repent and seek forgiveness from God and from those they have wronged.

Remember that God created you to be His child. There is nothing that could happen that would change His love for you. Because of this, you can love and respect yourself, too, and insist that others treat you with respect.

13

The New You

And just like that, you will continue to grow physically and in your relationships with other people of both sexes, with your family, and with God. The days and months and years just ahead of you are bright and exciting and so full of chances to use what God has given you.

The frustrations and disappointments will not end, but the joys and blessings will far outnumber them. You've reached the end of this book but not the end of learning about yourself and about others. Take these few reminders with you as you go on from here:

Do you think you will ever stop growing?

1. Accept yourself as a real and worthwhile gift from God. You are special and unique.
2. Work at your friendships. Reach out and help others. Be thoughtful toward them, and treat them the way you'd like to be treated.
3. Keep your body active and healthy. Take care of it since it's the only one you'll have. Eat wisely, take time for rest and recreation, develop your special interests, and use the gifts God has given you.
4. Improve your skills. Work at those areas in which you can achieve. Strengthen the weak spots. Decide to be the best you can be at whatever you try, accepting your strengths and your limits.
5. Share your thoughts and ideas with others. Talk to them. Ask for advice, and don't be afraid to risk being fair, just, and Christian. Open up to those you admire and trust. Be honest with your parents and friends.

6. Keep in touch with God. He's so close that you won't have to worry about getting His attention. Use regular church worship and Bible study as ways to grow in fellowship with God's people.

7. Accept your family just the way they are. Work to talk and to listen better. Forgive them and expect them to forgive you. Show them your love with words and with a hug now and then.

8. Continue to share God's love with others. Tell others about what you believe; tell them God loves them. God has put you here for that purpose too. Share the Good News any way you can.

9. Enjoy and celebrate life. Take your gift of sexuality eagerly, and use it the way God intended. Enter your maturity with joy; accept its challenges with excitement. Forgive as you have been forgiven. Practice "save sex until marriage" instead of "safe sex." There is no such thing as safe sex outside of marriage.

10. Remember that you are an important person—right now! God is with you and cares for you today. You are His, and He won't let you go. You can walk with confidence into the life that's waiting.

Why is it important to stay in touch with God?

Word List

Abortion (a-BOR-shun) Ending a pregnancy by killing the embryo or fetus.

Abstinence (AB-stin-ens) To refrain from sexual intercourse.

Adolescence (ad-uh-LES-sens) The period of life between childhood and adulthood; the teen years.

AIDS A sexually transmitted disease that breaks down a person's immune system, damaging the person's ability to fight other diseases.

Anus (AY-nes) The opening where bowel movements leave the body.

Cervix (SER-viks) The narrow outer end of the uterus.

Circumcision (ser-kum-SIZH-un) An operation that removes the foreskin from the end of the penis.

Clitoris (KLIT-or-is) A small organ at the front of the vaginal opening that gives sexual pleasure when touched.

Conceive (kon-SEEV) To start a new life through union of a sperm cell with an egg cell; to become pregnant.

Condom (KON-dom) A thin rubber sheath placed over the erect penis before intercourse to prevent sperm from entering the vagina. Because of its high rate of failure, it does not provide a "safe sex" prevention of sexually transmitted diseases, as is often claimed.

Ejaculation (ee-jack-yoo-LAY-shun) The discharge of semen from the penis.

Embryo (EM-bree-oh) The unborn baby during the first eight weeks after conception.

Erection (ee-RECK-shun) The enlarging and hardening of a male's penis, usually during sexual excitement.

Fallopian Tube (fa-LOW-pee-an TUBE) The passageway connecting each ovary to the uterus. The fertilizing of the egg by the sperm normally takes place here.

Fetus (FEE-tuss) The unborn baby after eight weeks or more in the mother's uterus.

Foreskin (FOR-skin) A fold of skin that covers the glans of the penis. (See Circumcision.)

Genital (JEN-i-tal) Pertaining to the sex organs.

Homosexuals (ho-mo-SEK-shoo-als) Men and women who, contrary to God's Word, prefer to satisfy their sexual desires with members of their own sex.

Hormone (HOR-mon) A product of living cells that circulates in the blood. Sex hormones affect the growth and function of the reproductive organs.

Hymen (HIGH-men) The thin membrane in a girl's body that covers the outside opening of the vagina.

Intercourse (IN-ter-corse) (See Sexual Intercourse.)

Labor (LAY-bur) The physical activities including contraction of the uterus and dilation of the cervix involved in giving birth.

Masturbation (mass-ter-BAY-shun) Sexual stimulation by handling or rubbing the genital organs.

Menstruation (men-stroo-AY-shun) The monthly flow of waste tissue and blood from the uterus. It is commonly called a *period.*

Miscarriage (MISS-care-idg) The process through which a mother's body expels a dead embryo or fetus.

Nocturnal Emission (nok-TER-nal ee-MISH-un) The release of semen during sleep, common in adolescent boys. Also called a "wet dream."

Orgasm (OR-gazm) A series of pleasurable muscular contractions centered in the sexual organs and affecting the entire body.

Ovary (OH-va-ree) The female reproductive organ in which egg cells develop and sex hormones are produced. Females have two ovaries.

Ovulation (AH-vyu-lay-shun) The discharge of a mature ovum from the ovary.

Ovum (OH-vum) The egg cell created in the female ovary and released during ovulation.

Penis (PEE-nis) The male sex organ that hangs between the legs and through which both urine and semen pass out of the body.

Period (See Menstruation.)

Pituitary Gland (pih-TOO-it-air-ee GLAND) The body's master gland located at the base of the brain. Its secretions control and regulate many organs and influence most basic body functions.

Placenta (pluh-SEN-ta) The organ that connects the fetus to the lining of the uterus by means of the umbilical cord.

Pornography (por-NOG-raf-ee) Books, movies, or videos that make sex dirty without a concern for God's Word or moral values.

Prostate Gland (PRAH-state GLAND) A male gland that secretes fluid that mixes with sperm.

Puberty (PYOO-ber-tee) The time of becoming physically mature and being capable of reproducing. This usually occurs between ages 13 and 16 in boys and 11 and 14 in girls.

Safe Sex The false idea that intercourse with appropriate "safeguards" such as condoms will keep people from getting a sexually transmitted disease. The only safe sex is with an uninfected partner in a marriage where husband and wife are faithful to each other.

Scrotum (SKRO-tum) A bag of skin that hangs from the groin between the legs of a male. It supports and protects the testicles.

Semen (SEE-men) The male fertilizing fluid that is made up of sperm and the whitish liquid in which they flow.

Sexual Abuse Being touched inappropriately by an adult or peer.

Sexual Intercourse (SEX-yool IN-ter-corse) The sexual union of a male and female; the inserting of the penis into the vagina.

Sexually Transmitted Disease (STD) Any of a variety of contagious diseases contracted almost entirely from sexual contact. The most common are AIDS, chlamydia, herpes, syphilis, human papilloma virus (HPV), and gonorrhea.

Sperm (SPERM) The male cell produced in the testicles to fertilize the female egg.

Sterility (STER-ill-it-ee) The inability to produce babies.

Testicles (TESS-ti-klz) The two egg-shaped male reproductive glands where sperm are produced.

Umbilical Cord (um-BIL-ih-kal KORD) The cord that connects the fetus to the placenta.

Urethra (yoo-REE-thra) The tube through which urine passes from the bladder out of the body. In males it also carries the semen.

Uterus (YOO-ter-us) Also called the womb. The place where the fertilized egg develops into a fully formed baby.

Vagina (vuh-JY-na) The passageway leading from the uterus to the vulva in a woman; the birth canal.

Virgin (VER-jin) A person who has never had sexual intercourse.

Vulva (VUL-va) The external female sex organ surrounding the genital opening.